D1552581

Plants of Old Hawaii

Warm Aloha,
Lois Lucas

PLANTS
OF
OLD HAWAII

by
LOIS LUCAS

with
illustrations by
Joan Fleming
and
poems by
Julie Williams

The Bess Press
P.O. Box 22388
Honolulu, HI 96822

Executive Editor: Ann Rayson
Design and Typography: Richard Wirtz

Library of Congress

CATALOG CARD NO.: 82-72199

Lucas, Lois
   Plants of Old Hawaii
Honolulu, Hawaii: Bess Press
112 pages   glossary, illustrations, bibliography

ISBN: 0-935848-11-8

Copyright © 1982 by The Bess Press
ALL RIGHTS RESERVED
Printed in the United States of America

Contents

Foreword

The literature of Hawaiiana has been growing rapidly over recent years. However, there has been a lack of schoolroom textbooks or learning aids of any kind in this field.

Lois Lucas, herself an elementary school teacher at Punahou, has now helped to fill this need with this study volume on the plants brought to these islands by the early Hawaiians. Through her experience, her vision, and her love of "things Hawaiian," she is bringing to the classroom a very important learning tool.

Her objective, as stated in her introduction, is to "create an atmosphere of love and concern, both on a teacher/student and student/student basis" for the rich heritage of Hawaiian culture, especially through study of the Hawaiians' close association with plants. In this unique book she has successfully and admirably succeeded in realizing her goal.

This is not merely a textbook for a teacher to use as a source for instruction, nor is it a schoolbook for students to study from—it is both of these and a lot more.

Plants of Old Hawaii is a plant science book about the twenty plants the original Hawaiians brought with them from the south Pacific circa 450 A.D. when they settled the Hawaiian islands. The book contains graphic illustrations by Joan Fleming of each plant and its flower and fruit, as well as plant descriptions, habitats, uses, legends, and proverbs. A poem about each plant by Julie Williams, a classroom teacher at the Kamehameha Schools, enhances the factual information provided by Lois Lucas and will delight the reader. Thus, *Plants of Old Hawaii* is a valuable resource book for all adult readers interested in Hawaiiana in addition to being *the* Hawaiian plant science book for students.

We are grateful to Lois Lucas for bringing to the classroom a rich experience in one phase of old Hawaiian culture.

Beatrice H. Krauss
H.L. Lyon Arboretum
The University of Hawaii
at Manoa

Acknowledgments

My deepest Mahalo to the many people who made this book possible.

First and foremost to Bea Krauss, who gave unstintingly of her knowledge, concern, and time to bring this material into fruition;

To Donald Kilolani Mitchell, who scanned the text for accurate information;

To Melissa Kim, whose dedicated interest in our Hawaiian Garden at Punahou motivated my work;

To Mahealani Pescaia, who brought an awareness to me of her effective use of the "ohana" teaching of social studies;

To Joan Fleming, who saw beauty in nature and with her talented pen translated it graphically for our children;

To Elaine Blitman, who encouraged consistency of form and designed the cover of *Plants of Old Hawaii;*

To Julie Stewart Williams of Kamehameha Schools, who wrote the wonderful poems on each plant;

To Marie Riley for narrative revision;

To Rick Wirtz for production and design;

To Ann Rayson for editing *Plants of Old Hawaii;*

And to my husband, Joseph T. Lucas, Jr. Md., for his patience.

Dedicated
to
my daughter
LANI

whose enthusiasm and knowledge spurred
me to "see" the beauty of Hawai'i

Introduction

I am presenting this book, not as an authority on botany, but as an elementary school teacher who realizes there is a great need for material to familiarize children with the environment in which they live and to help them appreciate the unique heritage that is Hawaii.

Through the exercise of certain skills, the primary goal of this book is to develop an attitude of appreciation for the environment and society of pre-contact Hawaii. By studying many of the most useful plants brought to Hawaii by the first Polynesian settlers, students will gain insights into the daily lives of the early Hawaiians. They will explore the physical skills, creativity, and art with which the Hawaiians adapted these plants to suit their needs without the use of clay or metal implements.

The basic philosophy of this book centers around the *'ohana* (family) concept. This concept can be explained with three Hawaiian words:

Aloha - love, concern

Kokua - help, assistance, comfort

Laulima - working together

Hopefully, the teacher will attempt to create an atmosphere of love and concern, both on a teacher/

student and a student/student basis. The teacher should also work to develop in the students the wish to help one another and the teamwork necessary for a meaningful learning experience. This philosophy or attitude will be the basis for the launching of all activities and discussions. The children will experience an atmosphere approximating that within which the Hawaiians lived. The students will then learn the concept of *Kapu,* religious beliefs, and the social roles assumed in the *Ahupua'a,* or the community.

This book is written at a middle elementary reading level. Words that might be considered difficult are printed in bold faced type in the text and defined in the Glossary. All Hawaiian words not found in the English dictionary are italicized except for proper names. In addition to the Glossary, there are bibliographies of Resources for both students and teachers and a pronunciation key of diacritical markings of Hawaiian words.

It is my sincere hope that *Plants of Old Hawaii* will become an integral part of your Hawaiiana curriculum and that you will find it to be a useful book.

COMMON NAME:	**Arrowroot**
HAWAIIAN NAME:	**PIA**

POEM:

PIA growing tall and straight,
  Its tubers we must pick and grate
For starch to mix with coconut cream
  To make huapia, in the imu to steam.

Julie Williams

HABITAT:

Arrowroot *(pia)* grows at low **altitudes,** in the open woods, and near a source of water.

DESCRIPTION:

Arrowroot *(pia)* is a member of the Tacca family. This plant had broad leaves. The leaves can measure one or more feet wide. The blades of these thin leaves are **cleft** into several parts. In winter, the leaves will die back.

The arrowroot plant grows from an underground root *(hua)*. In the spring, stems (**petioles**) will grow from the tubers to a length of one to two feet. The stems are marked with fine **grooves.** Many small flowers *(pua)* will appear at the top of the tall stems. These green and purple flowers may number three dozen or more.

The part of the arrowroot plant that people use is the **tuber.** It is a **carbohydrate,** a starch, which has several purposes.

USES:

The ancient Hawaiians used the arrowroot *(pia)* as a food and as a medicine. For food, they mixed the arrowroot with coconut cream or milk *(wai o ka nui)*, or wrapped it in tī *(kī)* leaves. Also they steamed the arrowroot in an *imu* to make the dessert *haupia*.

When the Hawaiians suffered from **diarrhea** they took arrowroot raw, with water. For **dysentery** they mixed the arrowroot with red clay. This contains much iron.

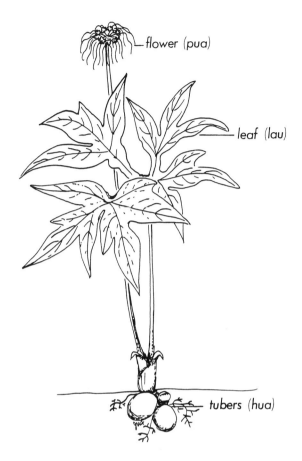

flower (pua)

leaf (lau)

tubers (hua)

Arrowroot

PIA

COMMON NAME:	Awa
HAWAIIAN NAME:	'AWA

HABITAT:

'Awa likes rain but not too much sun. Its habitat is the valleys of Hawai'i. In the valleys it can get the most moisture and the least sunshine.

DESCRIPTION:

'Awa is a member of the Pepper family. This plant grows from four to twelve feet tall. It is not a bushy plant because it does not grow many branches. It is straight and tall.

The leaves of the 'awa are heart-shaped. Very many flowers grow on a single stem. The smooth stems of the 'awa are green and have a slight bump or swelling at their nodes.

POEM:

The 'AWA is a shrub whose leaves
    Are shaped just like a heart,
A tranquilizer in the roots,
    Its most important part.

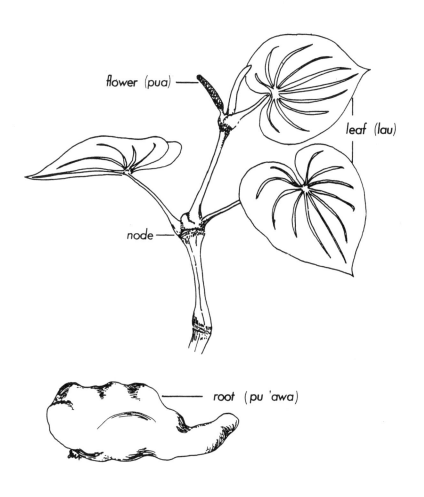

flower (pua)

leaf (lau)

node

root (pu 'awa)

Root portions one must chew or pound,
　　　With water mix, then strain,
A drink for ceremonies,
　　　To relax or lessen pain.

Julie Williams

USES:

　　　　　Laka, the goddess of the hula, liked the
'awa plant. At the hula school, the *hālau hula*, there was a
head student. This student, the *Po'o Pua'a,* carried the
'awa to the altar *(kuahu)* as a gift to Laka.
　　We call members of our family who lived long ago

our ancestors. The Hawaiians of old believed that their ancestors, *'aumākua,* guarded them. But sometimes the Hawaiians made these *'aumākua* angry. As punishment, the angry ancestors could make the Hawaiians sick. When the Hawaiians wanted to recover from this type of sickness, they made an offering of *'awa* to Laka. They believed that Laka would be pleased and would make them well again.

The Hawaiians worked very hard getting food and making their houses, canoes, clothing, dishes, and tools. Sometimes after hard work, the Hawaiians would have sore muscles. They made a drink from the *'awa* plant. This drink relieved the soreness. It also made the Hawaiians relaxed and sleepy. Sweet banana or sugar cane took away the bitter taste of the *'awa.*

Also the Hawaiians believed that the *'awa* leaves could cure a headache. They wrapped the leaves around their heads. Soon they would be well again. If a Hawaiian had a cough, he would make a drink from the root of the *'awa.* The Hawaiians believed that the *'awa* could take away many types of pain.

LEGEND:

"'*Awa* offered to a god was poured or sprinkled over the image, or, if there was no image, the *kahuna* sprinkled it in the air and drank the remainder in the cup. The cups used were always made of polished coconut shells cut lengthwise in the shape called *kānoa.* These cups were never placed on the floor itself but on a piece of *kapa* spread before the priest, never put where they might be stepped on or otherwise desecrated. As soon as the ceremony was over, they were washed, placed in a net *(kōkō),* and hung from the rafters. The strainer was also carefully washed and hung in the tree to dry. The order of serving also was important. At the entertainment of a guest, it was considered an insult to the host if the guest refused the cup or passed the cup handed to him, as guest of honor, to an inferior chief."*

---

*Martha Beckwith, *Hawaiian Mythology* (Honolulu, Hawaii: University of Hawaii Press, 1940), Page 94.

COMMON NAME:	**Bamboo**
HAWAIIAN NAME:	**ʻOHE**

HABITAT:

Bamboo *(ʻohe)* grows in forests where much rain falls. These forests are called "wet forests."

DESCRIPTION:

The bamboo plant *(ʻohe)* is a member of the Grass family. We can find bamboo plants growing in **dense** clumps. These clumps grow very tall, sometimes fifty feet high!

The bamboo may have green stems or yellow stems with green stripes. A small bamboo stem measures two inches in **diameter,** and a large stem measures four inches in **diameter.** Parts of bamboo stems are hollow. Because they are hollow, air can move through them. Air moving through a piece of bamboo can make a musical sound.

The hollow parts of a bamboo stem look like long tubes. They have very thin walls. We call the thin-walled, hollow sections of the bamboo the **internodes.** A bamboo plant has many **internodes.** The places where the internodes join each other are called the **nodes.** The nodes are hard and thick; they are not hollow at all.

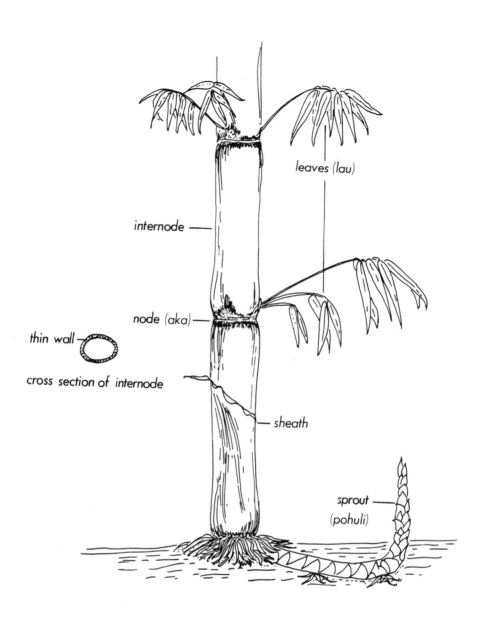

leaves (lau)

internode

node (aka)

thin wall

cross section of internode

sheath

sprout
(pohuli)

Which part of the bamboo would make a good instrument, the nodes or the internodes?

The bamboo plant also has green leaves. The leaves grow about fourteen inches long and two inches wide. Most leaves are smaller than this. The tough **margins** and undersides of the leaves can cut our fingers if we grab at them and pull.

POEM:

> Hawaiian bamboo's narrow leaves
> And long joints can be seen,
> One kind with stripes of green on gold
> The other, only green.
>
> The thin-walled stems are fringed
> So that pū'ili can be made,
> With puka made into the sides
> A nose flute can be played.

Julie Williams

USES:

The ancient Hawaiians used the hollow tubes of bamboo stems to blow air on their fires. The air makes the fire grow stronger. They also used the tubes to make musical instruments.

The Hawaiians played a nose flute, called *'ohe-hano-ihu*. They made it from the hollow stem of the bamboo. Because air moves through the flute, it belongs to the family of wind instruments.

The Hawaiians also made **percussion** instruments from the hollow stems of the bamboo. "**Percussion**" means that the instruments are hit to create the musical sounds. The Hawaiians hit hollow pieces of bamboo together to accompany their dance, the hula *('ohe kā'eke'eke* or *kā 'eke'eke pahūpahū)*. They also used a fringed bamboo tube that would rattle when hit *(pū'ili* or *hula pū'ili)*.

A hula dancer moved to the beat of the instrument. Bamboo could make many different sounds. Short pieces of bamboo made one sound, and longer pieces made other sounds. Some tubes were wide in diameter; some were narrow. Some tubes had a closed end, and some were open. Each piece of bamboo created a different sound.

From the bamboo, the Hawaiians made fishing rods. Long pieces of bamboo also became the frame for the house *(hale)*. Racing sleds, as well, needed a frame made from the bamboo. Bamboo made a light frame for the *hale* and for the sleds.

Bamboo helped the Hawaiians carry water. Tubes with a closed end could become water carriers. Also, the Hawaiians learned to move water by cutting the bamboo in half down its long side. They then carved out the thick middle of the nodes. Water could run along these pieces of bamboo to the Hawaiians' crops. The bamboo helped the Hawaiians to irrigate their crops.

Knives to cut soft materials were made from the bamboo. Very thin pieces of bamboo became needles. The Hawaiians used these needles to string *kukui* nuts for candles *(kalikukui)*.

The bamboo helped the Hawaiians make designs on the *kapa*. The sticks of bamboo could make lines with dye on the *kapa*. These sticks for drawing are called *lapa*. Hawaiians also cut designs in other sticks of bamboo. They dipped the sticks into the dye and stamped a pattern on the *kapa*. These stamps made of bamboo they called *'ohe-kapala*. The *lapa* and the *'ohe-kapala* were kept in a case also made of bamboo.

LEGENDS:

Hina, a widely known goddess or demigoddess of many Polynesian legends, was in one legend the wife of Akalana and mother of Maui. She brought *'ohe* from Kahiki and planted it beside her door. When Maui saw the plant, he reached for it. The sharp stem of the bamboo cut his hand. Hina, who was a powerful goddess, then turned the stem inside out. Now the sharp part of the bamboo is inside the stem. The outside is smooth and round.

When Laukia'i'ai, guardian of food, wanted to find her father, she sat down on a piece of bamboo. It grew and grew. Finally it bent over and set her down in a place far away. There she found her father.

A RIDDLE:

A container, a lid.	He nane
A container, a lid.	He ipu no, he po'i
What is it?	He ipu no, he po'i
	Ka'ohe.

Answer: the bamboo ('ohe).

| COMMON NAME: | **Banana** |
| HAWAIIAN NAME: | **MAI`A** |

POEM:

Seventy different MAI`A
Grown in days of old,
Sixty-eight reserved for men,
For women, two, all told.

Banana leaves are useful,
'Specially as a cover,
For food and sandals and for shrines
And one thing or another.

Vitamins for babies
From the juice of flower tips,
And from the juice of flower buds,
A dye for kapa strips.

Julie Williams

HABITAT:

The banana *(mai'a)* grows well in moist areas away from the wind. It likes to grow in gulches on the lower **fringe** of a forest. There it is protected. You can find the *mai'a* growing between the **altitudes** of 1500 feet and 3000 feet.

DESCRIPTION:

The banana *(mai'a)* is a member of the Banana family. It is really a remarkable plant. Most people think that the banana is a tree, but it is not a tree. It is really a giant herb. A tree has a large stem, which we call a tree trunk. The banana plant has no **aerial** stem, or trunk above the ground for most of its life. Instead it has a stem underground, like the stem of the taro.

Part of the banana plant above the ground looks like a stem, but it is really a tight stalk of leaves. These leaves grow up straight from the underground stem. The young leaves grow in the center of the sheath of older leaves. The young leaves must push the older leaves aside to make room for themselves and form a series of **crescents** that look like an onion in cross section. The stalk becomes thicker as more and more new leaves push from the center. The banana plant will grow from eight to twenty-five feet tall.

Many fruit grow on a single stalk of the banana plant. When these bananas are **mature,** someone will cut down the whole plant, not just the stalk, for this plant is now dead.

Bananas in Hawai'i have no seeds, so we can't plant a seed to grow a new banana plant after the dead stalk has been cut down. But if we look around the dead plant, we will see *keiki* stalks already growing from the underground stem. These young stalks are called **suckers.** Each **sucker** will develop into another banana plant. In time, it

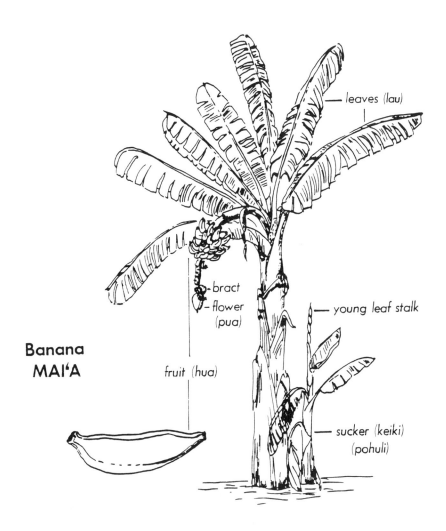

Banana
MAI‘A

leaves (lau)

bract
flower
(pua)

young leaf stalk

fruit (hua)

sucker (keiki)
(pohuli)

too will produce fruit for cutting and eating.

The banana plant has long leaves. Veins in a leaf will give it strength. The leaves of the banana *(mai‘a)* have prominent veins running the width, but they do not have veins running the length. For this reason, the wind can easily tear the banana leaves across their width. The torn leaves then appear to have many segments as they flap in the wind.

The banana plant prepares for its fruit by developing a cup-like structure. This brownish-red cup is called a **bract.** It will curl back as the banana plant prepares to flower. Often the perfect flowers develop into the banana plant's fruit.

It takes almost a year for the crop of bananas to **mature**. Banana fruit grow in rows; a row is called a "hand" of bananas. We buy bananas in a "hand" at the grocery store. Each banana plant will bear five to nine hands of fruit. The Hawaiians of old had 70 or more varieties of bananas *(mai'a)*.

The skin of the ripe fruit ranges in color from yellow to green. The pulp of the fruit may be yellow, pink, salmon, or almost white. If the ripe fruit is eaten raw, it is a sugar. However, it becomes a starch when cooked.

USES:
The ancient Hawaiians had many uses for the banana plant. For one, they could wave a young plant as a sign of truce in a war.

With the blade of a leaf, the Hawaiians could make an umbrella. They could also create a wrapper for anything needing protection.

The leaf sheath, or false stem, could also become a wrapper. Sometimes this wrapper served to keep leis fresh. Other times, this sheath could hold food to be steamed in the *imu.* It could become a backing for a lei *(haku),* or it could be used to string a common lei *(kui).* When beaten, it could serve as *kapa,* but not a good quality *kapa.*

Sections of the banana sheath fit together to make water pipes. The sheath was even strong enough to be used for temporary sandals.

The flower of the banana plant *(mai'a)* also served the ancient Hawaiians. From the flower tips the Hawaiians obtained honey. They used this honey as a vitamin for their babies. The juice of the flower buds became a dye, and the juice from the root was used to treat thrush *('ea)* in the babies' mouths.

The ancient Hawaiians considered the banana fruit a delicacy. Chiefs and priests ate the banana at feasts. Only in famine did the banana become a **staple**. Women in ancient Hawai'i were forbidden to eat most bananas. Only one or two kinds could they eat.

INTERESTING INFORMATION:

In sacrifices to the gods, sometimes the ancient Hawaiians substituted a banana stalk for a human.

LEGENDS:

Long ago all bananas bore their fruit on upright stems like the mountain banana. The lowlands and the mountain banana quarreled and fought. The lowlanders were defeated, and to this day bananas hang their heads in shame.

According to another Hawaiian legend, the brother of Pele, goddess of volcanoes, brought the banana to Hawai'i. In Hawai'i the people believe that it is bad luck to dream of bananas, or to meet a person carrying them, or to carry bananas for lunch on a fishing trip.

PROVERB:

"A man is like a banana stalk who falls easily," or "A man is like a banana, bearing fruit in good time."

COMMON NAME:	# Breadfruit
HAWAIIAN NAME:	# 'ULU

HABITAT:

The breadfruit *('ulu)* grows in hot, moist places.

DESCRIPTION:

The breadfruit *('ulu)* is a member of the Mulberry family. It is a tall tree of striking appearance. It may grow to heights of 30 feet. The **diameter** of the breadfruit trunk can measure up to three or four feet.

The foliage is beautiful and **luxuriant.** The tree has very large leaves one to three feet long. The leaves are usually **lobed.** The male flowers and the female flowers grow separately on the same tree. The male flowers are crowded on a large, club-shaped, yellow **catskin;** the female flowers appear on a large, rounded **receptacle.**

The fruit develops from the female flower. The large fruit may be five to eight inches in diameter and may weigh up to ten pounds! This fruit is not a single fruit as you would believe when you first look at it. It is really a

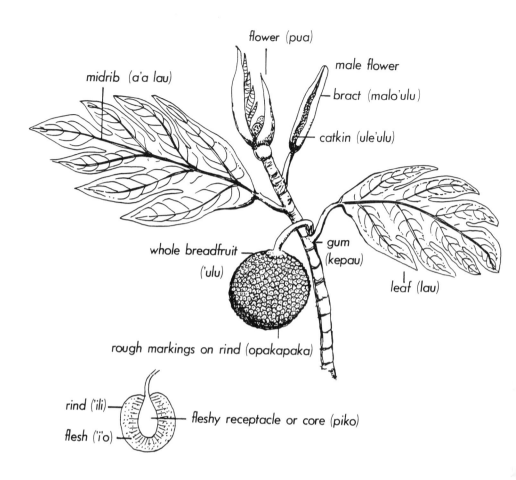

flower (pua)

midrib (a'a lau)

male flower

bract (malo'ulu)

catkin (ule'ulu)

whole breadfruit ('ulu)

gum (kepau)

leaf (lau)

rough markings on rind (opakapaka)

rind ('ili)

fleshy receptacle or core (piko)

flesh ('i'o)

collection of many smaller fruits pressing against each other. They press with such force that they almost lose their **identity**. This type of fruit is called a composite or collective fruit.

Study the **diagram** closely to see how the fruit is constructed. Do you see the core? Each small fruit is attached to this core. The outside of the whole fruit is covered with a "warty" skin or rind. Inside you will find a sweet pulp, somewhat like a sweet potato. The breadfruit (*'ulu*) is a **carbohydrate**, a starch.

IMPORTANT INFORMATION:

Some varities of this plant are not able to produce seeds. Thus the breadfruit depends upon man. Man must plant cuttings of the root shoots to get new trees. For this reason, the 'ulu is often found close to people's houses.

POEM:

The 'ULU is a beautiful tree,
 With big round breadfruit very easy to see;
Boards for surfing and pounding poi,
 Drums for beating by man or boy.

Caulking and glue from the milky sap,
 Spread on branches, certain birds to trap,
Dried leaf sheath for sandpaper fine,
 To polish kukui nuts and bowls to dine.

Julie Williams

USES:

The ancient Hawaiians used all parts of the breadfruit in their daily lives. With the trunk of the 'ulu, the Hawaiians made drums *(pahu)* to accompany the hula. Also they shaped surfboards *(papa he'e nalu)* from the 'ulu trunk. The light wood of the breadfruit made good surfboards.

Poi boards *(papa ku'i 'ai)* were made from the breadfruit tree trunk. For the bows, stem pieces, and gunwales of their canoes, the Hawaiians also used wood of the 'ulu.

The **bract** *(malo 'ulu)* served as an **abrasive**. As a fine sandpaper, it helped the Hawaiians to polish bowls and kukui nuts for decoration.

The Hawaiians prepared food from the 'ulu in many ways. In the *imu* they baked the breadfruit. They could peel the skin off or leave it on. With a sliver of bamboo they removed the core of the 'ulu.

The Hawaiians could pound the breadfruit to make poi. This poi was not as good as that made from the *kalo* plant. We call this **inferior** poi. The Hawaiians could also make a pudding from the breadfruit *(pepeie'e 'ulu)*. They mixed the very ripe fruit with coconut milk. Then they wrapped the pudding in ti *(kī)* leaves, and baked it in an *imu,* or dried it in the sun for later use.

Even the breadfruit peelings served the Hawaiians. The Hawaiians fattened their pigs with the peelings and scraps.

From the breadfruit tree stem comes a latex (gum). The Hawaiian children chewed this gum. It also served as a glue. The glue could join two gourds to make a gourd drum. In the seams of canoes, the Hawaiians spread the gum to keep water out.

The Hawaiians used a gum *(pīlali'ulu)* from the milky sap of the breadfruit to catch birds. When the birds' feet stuck to the gum, the Hawaiians could pluck the feathers they needed. They then could dissolve the gum with *kukui* nut oil to set the bird free.

The same gum was used to cure skin diseases. Also, the leaf buds cured thrush *('ea),* a disease of the mouth of young children and babies.

LEGENDS:

Niheu, a hero, was much too mischievous to please the gods. He especially angered them when he stole a breadfruit *('ulu).* One of the gods had used the breadfruit to roll and thunder across the floor of the underworld.

PROVERBS:

"When bread fruit is ripe
(Hua ka 'ulu
The squid comes in."
ku mai ka he'e)

"He will become a breadfruit that oozes gum," refers to a newly rich person.

COMMON NAME:	**Candlenut**
HAWAIIAN NAME:	**KUKUI**

POEM:

The beautiful leaves of KUKUI trees
    Show a silvery ruffle with every breeze;
For they remember, legend tells everyone,
    That first to give light was the moon,
        Not the sun.

Roast the nuts and in the kernel
    Is a lot of oil,
Lighting torches, lamps, and candles
    After a day of toil.

Break the green nut from the stem,
    The sap you see can seal,
By placing it upon a wound,
    It helps the wound to heal.

A child with thrush or coated tongue,
    You rub the sap within;
But well kids chew the tree trunk's gum
    While playing games to win.

In many, many other ways
    Our state tree can be used:
Clearing ocean water
    So Fishermen won't be confused;
Hard shells polished shiny smooth,
    A lei can soon be made,
As well as lovely colors,
    Four dyes of varying shade;
A stain for nets unseen by fish,
    A finish for canoes;
Kernels roasted for 'inamona,
    A relish for pūpūs.

Julie Williams

HABITAT:

    The candlenut *(kukui)* grows in valleys and gulches.

DESCRIPTION:

    The candlenut *(kukui)* is a member of the Spurge family. The trunk is smooth, straight, and unbranched to a height of forty feet or more.

If we look at the hillsides of most gulches, we can easily spot the *kukui* tree. The light color of its leaves contrasts with the other, darker trees and plants. These light green leaves are covered with silvery gray powder. Clusters of small flowers will appear at the end of the branches.

The candlenut *(kukui)* fruit has two shapes. If the fruit bears one seed, it is round. If the fruit contains two seeds, it is **elliptical.** The **immature** fruit has a hard green covering about ¼ inch thick. As the fruit **matures,** it turns a dark gray-black and becomes soft. The fruit is especially soft after it has fallen to the ground.

Inside this husk we will find a nut. The nut is white

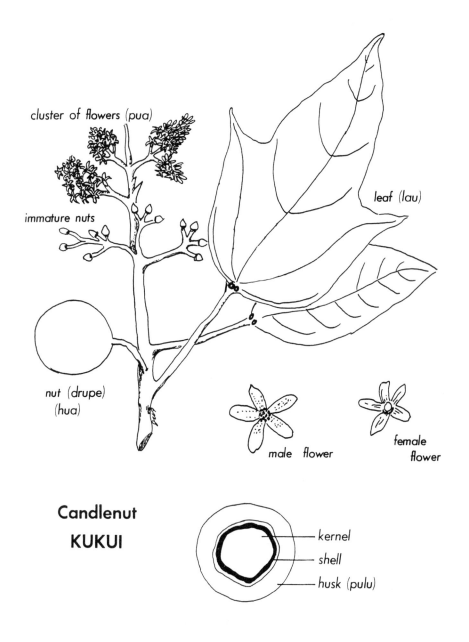

cluster of flowers (pua)

leaf (lau)

immature nuts

nut (drupe)
(hua)

male flower

female
flower

Candlenut
KUKUI

kernel

shell

husk (pulu)

when it is young. White *kukui* nut leis are made from young nuts. However, when the nut **matures,** its shell becomes black. It is very hard, thick, and "wrinkled." The wrinkled look comes from the many **grooves** in the nut. Inside this nut, or coat, is the seed meat, or kernel. The kernel is rich with oil.

USES:

The *kukui* was an important source of dye for the ancient Hawaiians. From this tree, the Hawaiians could obtain colors from copper red to black for dying their *kapa*. The bark gave them a brown color. From the roots they got a black dye. The charred nut shells and the soot from burned nuts also gave a black dye.

The kernel of the *kukui* served the Hawaiians very well. It could be roasted, pounded and mixed with salt to become *inamona*, a relish which Hawaiians liked to eat.

In their households the Hawaiians relied upon the *kukui* nut oil. The Hawaiians roasted the *kukui* nuts and removed the kernels from the hulls. With a short piece of the **midrib** *(ni'au)* of coconut *(niu)* leaf, they strung the kernels to make a large torch *(lamakū)*. They also strung the kernels on a long sliver of bamboo *('ohe)* to make a candle *(īhoiho kukui)*. The burning oil in the kernel created light.

The string of kernels was set against a stone and lighted. One of the Hawaiian children tended the candle. After the upper kernel had burned away, the child turned the candle to make the remaining flame light the next kernel. Each kernel burned for three minutes.

For a brighter light, the Hawaiians made a torch of bamboo *('ohe)*. They stuffed the hollow bamboo with roasted kernels and burned them. This torch they called a *lama*.

Fishing was central to the Hawaiian life, and the *kukui* helped the Hawaiians fish. From the white, soft wood of the tree, the Hawaiians built a canoe buoy *(ama)*. This buoy would last for one year. For their fishnet floats *('ikoi* and *lana)*, the Hawaiians also used the *kukui* wood. The fishermen even chewed *kukui* kernels.

The men would blow the pieces out of their mouths over the sea. The oil from the kernels would make the waters quiet enough to see squid. The oil from the kernel of the *kukui* was also used to polish.

Hawaiian fishermen needed to make their fishnets strong. They could not allow these nets to decay. From the liquid of the *kukui's* inner bark, the Hawaiians made a stain to protect their nets. They pounded the inner bark of an old tree and strained the liquid. Then they dipped their nets in the liquid. When the nets were dry, the Hawaiians repeated the dipping. Hawaiians who used their nets frequently dipped the nets in *kukui* every six months.

The candlenut *(kukui)* served too as a medicine. If a Hawaiian had cut or punctured his skin, he could seal the cut with juice from the green *kukui* nut. 'Ea, the mouth disease of the children, could be treated with the *kukui* sap.

Kukui blossoms, bark, or the charcoal from burned nuts could be added to certain medicines. The raw *kukui* nut was **cathartic**. Sometimes a person could take too much of the raw nut. Then he would have to eat poi or starch *(pia)* to become well again.

The polished *kukui* nut made a nice ornament for the ancient Hawaiians. They wore the nuts around their necks or on their wrists.

To catch a criminal, the ancient Hawaiian priests used these nuts in the fire. Each time a nut was put in the fire, the priest would ask for the wrongdoer to admit his crime. As he burned the third nut, the priest asked for the last time. If no one confessed the crime, the priest said prayers for punishment of the criminal. Usually the wrongdoer would then suffer from great guilt. The wrongdoer believed that the prayer of the priest would bring punishment from the gods, and so it did. The guilt and fear were the punishment.

LEGENDS:

Kaula married Kekele, whose breath and skin were as sweet as the food made of the *kukui.*

The *menehune,* or little people, made tops of the *kukui* nut.

When Makali'i, god of plenty, was unable to see the shark that had swallowed his brother, he chewed some *kukui* nut and spat it on the water. The *kukui* oil caused the water to clear.

Moemoe desired only to sleep. One day while he was having a long nap, a stream rose and covered him with debris. Only his nose stuck out. On his nose a *kukui* nut rested and began to grow. It tickled his nostrils. Moemoe woke up angrily and cried, "Here I am in my favorite pastime and I am awakened by this cursed *kukui* tree." He gave up trying to sleep and, we assume, began a useful life.

PROVERBS:

"The gum sticks to the candlenut tree" refers to a parasite or a child clinging to his mother.

"When the *kukui* nut is spat on the water, the sea is smooth." This saying means the same as "pouring oil on troubled waters."

Coconut

NIU

HABITAT:

The coconut tree *(niu)* is a **strand** plant. It grows best on the warmer, leeward sides of the islands of Hawai'i. Its trunk may be seen standing within reach of the ocean spray. It may also grow at higher elevations. The coconut *(niu)* may live sixty to seventy years. An occasional coconut tree may live one hundred years or longer!

DESCRIPTION:

The coconut *(niu)* is a member of the Palm family. It is a graceful, tall palm; the slender trunk rises as much as one hundred feet from the thick base. The base does not rise straight up from the ground. Instead it is **inclined** to one side to ride the wind better. During the so-called Kona storms that sometimes strike the Islands, the slender trunks lean far toward the ground before heavy gusts. After each gust has passed, the trees will spring back to their original position.

From the time that the tree reaches ten years old until its death, it will continually produce clusters of flowers. These tiny flowers need protection, so the coconut tree *(niu)* will enclose them in a very large green structure called the **spathe**. When the flowers become large, they will burst the **spathe**. Ten months after they burst out, the flowers develop into fruit known as the coconut. The coconut fruit has a large seed protected by a thick husk. We have to work hard to break open the husk to find the seed. One end of the seed has three spots on the surface called "eyes." A liquid called milk fills the young shell.

The trunk is **surmounted** by a massive crown of leaves, of which the lower have a tendency to **droop**. These leaves are 10 to 20 feet long and bear approximately 100 leaflets on each side.

The coconut tree *(niu)* was one of the most valuable plants that the ancient Hawaiians brought with them.

USES:

The coconut provided the Hawaiians with food. The sweet milk of the coconut gave them a germ-free drink. The Hawaiians did not have to boil the milk to make it pure. They could husk the young coconut and drink its milk right on the spot. As the coconut matures, pulp begins to form on the inner surface of the shell. We call this pulp "meat." That meat at first looks like a custard. We can eat it with a spoon. by the second stage, the meat resembles a white cheese. The Hawaiians ate it on tī *(kī)*. Later on, the meat becomes firm. At this third stage, the Hawaiians grated the coconut meat for their food. They squeezed the grated coconut to mix with greens for their main dishes. They also made a dessert-like pudding *(haupia)* from the squeezed meat.

In Hawaiian households, the coconut had a number of uses. The Hawaiians could plait the stiff leaflets to make baskets used to carry food. With stiff midribs tied together at the base, the Hawaiians could create a broom *(pūlumi niʻau)*. On the coconut midribs, the Hawaiians

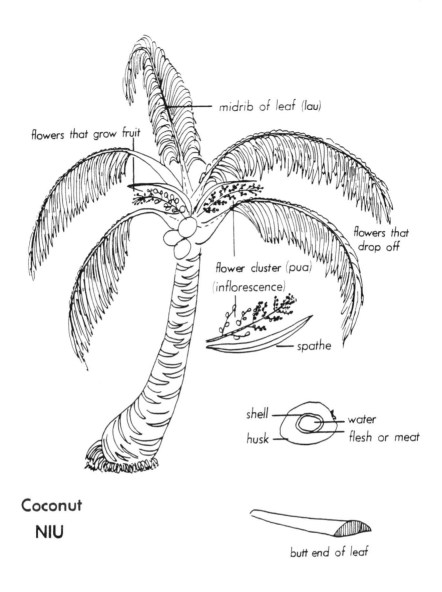

midrib of leaf (lau)

flowers that grow fruit

flowers that drop off

flower cluster (pua)
(inflorescence)

spathe

shell

water

husk

flesh or meat

Coconut
NIU

butt end of leaf

also threaded *kukui* kernels *(nī'au)* to make a candle *(lama kū)*. For a strainer, the Hawaiians took a clean piece of fibrous material *('a'a)* found at the base of the leaf cluster of the coconut tree. This material looks like nature's weaving, for it has many holes in it. The Hawaiians could strain a liquid through this material.

When they needed a rake, the Hawaiians used a dried flower cluster from the coconut.

The shells *('umeke pūniu)* of the coconut fruit became

containers for the ancient Hawaiians. The shells could be cut lengthwise or crosswise, at a right angle to the grain. The shells cut lengthwise were called *olo.* These were used by the priests. The shell containers cut at right angles were called *'apu-niu,* and they were used by the people. The coconut gave the Hawaiians tied wooden handles to part of a small coconut shell to make these ladles.

In their entertainment, the Hawaiians also used the coconut. The large drum *(pahu)* was made from a hollow coconut tree trunk. To create a knee drum *(pūniu),* the Hawaiians used the end of the coconut shell with the three "eyes." They smoothed and polished the shell. Then they covered the opening with the skin of a fish *(kala)* which had no scales. The Hawaiians placed the skin over the opening when the skin was still moist. To fasten the skin to the shell they used the gum *(pīlali)* from the *kukui* tree. When the fish skin dried, it became very taut and became a good surface for a drum.

The Hawaiians made another instrument called *ni'au kani* from the midribs of the coconut leaf. The player of this instrument kept the ends of the midribs between his teeth. When he struck the midribs, they vibrated between his teeth and made a musical sound.

Two games, *palai'ie* and *pana panan i'au,* used braided coconut fiber. Children tried to catch the *kapa* ball in a coconut fiber loop.

Fiber from the coconut husk could be braided and twisted into strong cord. This cord we call sennet, and the ancient Hawaiians called *'aha.* With the cord the Hawaiians could tie the handle *('au)* to the adz *(ko'i).* They could also tie the seams of a canoe together with sennit *('aha).* Nets *(kōkō)* to carry calabashes or other utensils were also made of sennit. Sennit also served to lash the outrigger to the canoe.

POEM:

> In all the world the palm best known
>> Is graceful Coco Palm,
> A symbol of Hawai'i nei
>> On shores by ocean calm.
>
> Of all the plants it was the NIU
>> That gave Hawaiians the most,
> The trunk could make a hula drum,
>> A calabash or post.
>
> The leaves made thatching for a house
>> Sometimes a fan or game,
> Long fibers of the husks made cordage
>> Called "sennit," that's its name.
>
> The midribs of the leaflets
>> Were bunched to make a broom,
> Or poked through kukui kernels
>> For lighting up a room.
>
> The fiber at the leaf stem base
>> A strainer it could make,
> And for a man, a malo, or
>> Sandals he could take.
>
> The nut provides both food and drink
>> Its water is so sweet,
> But just how old the nut is
>> Determines the use of the meat.
>
> When young the meat is very soft
>> You eat it raw, no need to steam,
> When old it's grated, squeezed, and strained
>> For 'ono coconut cream.

From the shell came spoons and bowls
And various containers,
It also made a small knee drum
For use by entertainers.

Julie Williams

LEGEND:

There was once a magic coconut palm concealed under a calabash. When the queen removed the cover, the tree grew and carried her off to heaven. There she could talk with her grandfather who lived in the sky.

RIDDLES:

Three walls and you reach water.
    What is it?
A man with three eyes; he can cry out of only one,
    What is it?
Something goes up brown and comes down white.
    What is it?
My sweet-water spring suspended in air.
    What is it?

Answer: The coconut (*niu*).

	Bottle
	(or White-Flowered)
COMMON NAME:	Gourd
HAWAIIAN NAME:	IPU

POEM:

Keeping time to the IPU beat,
    Dancers sway and move their feet;
Hula drums some IPU make,
    Or water gourds on trips to take.

For storing things like kapa fine,
    For carrying fishermen's hooks and line;
For bailing water from canoes,
    For masks and even food bowls, too.

Julie Williams

HABITAT:

The bottle gourd *(ipu)* will grow in dry areas. This vine needs a natural or man-made support. A natural support for the *ipu* would be a tree; a man-made support would be a post.

DESCRIPTION:

Gourd *(ipu)* is a member of the Gourd family. It is a wide-spreading vine with branched **tendrils**. The leaves of the *ipu* are shaped like hearts. They will grow from four to sixteen inches in diameter. Each leaf has five **lobes**. At night, small white flowers bloom on this vine. The flowers measure only one and one-half inches in length.

The young fruit of *ipu* is soft and covered with downy hairs. As the fruit *matures,* it becomes smooth. This fruit may be **mottled** green, or it may be white. It also takes various shapes. A gourd fruit may be **elliptical,** round, club-shaped, crooked, or twisted! It can grow short and thick, or it can grow long and thin. This fruit of the gourd *(ipu)* contains a white pulp and flat seeds. The light-colored seeds are about one-half inch long.

USES:

The gourd *(ipu)* was very useful to the ancient Hawaiians. The dried shell of the *ipu* made an excellent container. In this container made from *ipu,* the Hawaiians kept food, water, and dyes. They also used it to hold clothing, shark bait, and fishhooks.

Gourds also became musical instruments. Small, pear-shaped gourds could become whistles *(ipu hōkiokio).* The Hawaiians also made rattles from the *ipu ('uli'uli).* The Hawaiians could create a simple rattle with a straight handle which had a decorated circular cover. For the hula, the Hawaiians made drums from the gourd *(ipu hula).* They joined two gourds together, with the

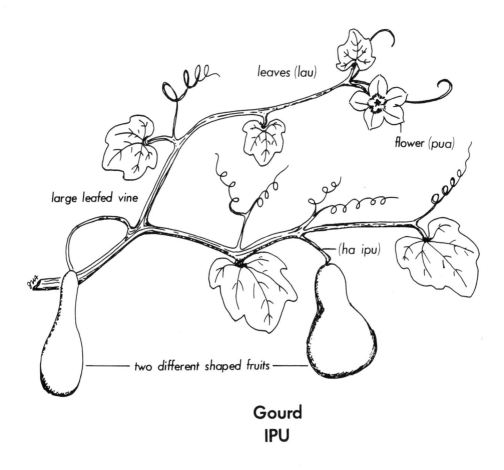

leaves (lau)

flower (pua)

large leafed vine

(ha ipu)

two different shaped fruits

Gourd
IPU

smaller one on top of the larger one.

The gourd *(ipu)* shell also served as a rat guard on the legs of the temple offering stand *(lele)*. A guard on each leg kept rats from climbing up on the stand to eat the food prepared for the gods.

Hawaiian fishermen used the gourd *(ipu)* to chase away sharks. With the *ipu* the fishermen could make sounds which frightened sharks.

LEGENDS:

Legends often tell how a god who has lived on earth takes at death the form of a plant. Legend tells this about the gourd *(ipu)* vine:

"A chieftess of a certain family dies and is buried in a cave. From her navel grows a gourd vine. It finds its way to the garden of a chief ... and there produces a fine gourd. The chief thumps it to test its ripeness, and the spirit of the gourd complains to a *kahuna* in a dream. *Kahuna* and chief trace the vine to its source, and the gourd is thereafter treated respectfully."

---

* Green and Pukui, *Legends of Kawelo and Other Hawaiian Folktales* (Honolulu, Hawaii: University of Hawaii Press, 1936), page 156.

COMMON NAME:	**Hau**
HAWAIIAN NAME:	**HAU**

POEM:

So many uses for the HAU,
    Like an outrigger boom and a fire plow,
A massage stick and a lightweight spear,
    So warriors can practice and have no fear.

The wood is tough but rather light,
    For fish net floats and the frame of a kite,
A yellow flower with center so dark,
    Cordage twisted from the inner bark.

Julie Williams

HABITAT:

This spreading tree grows in moist areas, from the beach up to 2000 feet of elevation.

DESCRIPTION:

Hau is a member of the Hibiscus family. It is a strong but very light-weighted wood. It grows low to the ground and has many branches. These branches are **horizontal** or nearly **horizontal** to the trunk. As the tree spreads, its branches intertwine. The branches create an impenetrable tangle. It is a strong but very lightweight wood.

The *hau* leaves are broad and heart-shaped. Sometimes the leaves are **scalloped.** They vary in size from two to twelve inches in diameter. When we touch the leaves, we notice that they are smooth on the upper surface, and white and velvety on the underside. The feel of velvet comes from the matted hairs in this area.

Near the tips of the branches, flowers will grow. These flowers look like hibiscus flowers. The petals are a bright yellow. The center may be brown or dark red. As the day lengthens, the colors change to dull orange. By night, the color may be a dull red. The petals drop to the ground the next morning.

There is fruit on this tree. The fruit is dry, brown, and downy. It has an oval shape.

IMPORTANT INFORMATION:

Hau was very highly valued by the ancient Hawaiians. No *commoner* could cut any *hau* branches without first getting permission from the chief.

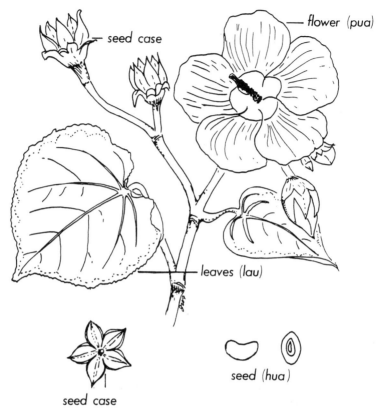

seed case

flower (pua)

leaves (lau)

seed (hua)

seed case

HAU

USES:

From the trunk or inner bark of the *hau*, the Hawaiians made a cord. This cord had many practical uses. For one, it provided a handle for gourds which carried water. The *hau* cord also fastened the covers of *lauhala* baskets. With the cord, the Hawaiians sewed the *kapa* bedsheets together and tied their sandals on their feet.

Not all the designs on the *kapa* were made with

bamboo sticks *(lapa)*. Some designs came about through the use of *hau* cord. The Hawaiians dipped the cord into the dye and then snapped it against the *kapa (kaula ho'olu'u kapa)*.

The Hawaiians needed to pull the *koa* logs for their canoes from the forest to the sea. To do so, they used strong rope made from braided *(hilo) hau*. When the Hawaiians fished for *mālolo,* flying fish, they used *hau* to tie ropes to the net of the bag.

Weapons too were created with *hau* cord. The cord could serve as the string of a bow, or as the sling of a slingshot. The Hawaiians also learned to thread a *hau* cord with sharks' teeth. This created a striking string for a weapon. The *hau* also held sharpened spear points onto the shafts of the spears. The Hawaiians used these spears in war and in sports.

The branches of *hau* served many uses. The Hawaiians could set the branches up along a shoreline to indicate *kapu* fishing zones. In these zones the fish were **spawning.** The Hawaiians wanted to protect the **spawning** fish.

The outrigger booms *('iako)* were made from *hau* branches. Why do you think the Hawaiians used the *hau* for an outrigger boom *('iako)*? The shape of *hau* was such that all they had to do was peel off the outer bark, soak it in sea water, clean it smoothly, and polish the finished boom.

The outrigger floats *(ama)* were also made from *hau*. Kites, which needed lightweight wood, had frames made of *hau* branches *(ho'lele lupe)*. Adz handles *('au)* too were shaped from the light wood of *hau*.

LEGENDS:

Hawaiian legend says that the *hau* is the visible form of the *manoa* wind.

Another myth states that the sister of Hina was changed into a *hau* tree.

COMMON NAME:	**Indian Mulberry**
HAWAIIAN NAME:	**NONI**

HABITAT:

We can find the Indian Mulberry *(noni)* growing in open lowlands and in the open forest.

DESCRIPTON:

Indian Mulberry *(noni)* is a member of the Coffee family. It is a small evergreen tree or shrub; rarely does it grow to twenty feet. Its branches are coarse and **angular.**

The leaves of *noni* are large, shiny, and oval. They grow from the branch in pairs except where the fruit forms. There we will find one leaf and one fruit. The leaves of *noni* grow eight inches or longer; they have many veins and very short stems.

The flowers of *noni* grow in heads. Each head contains many flowers, and each flower consists of five to seven white petals. These petals are shaped like small tubes, and they measure only one-third inch long.

The Indian Mulberry *(noni)* bears a small, pale

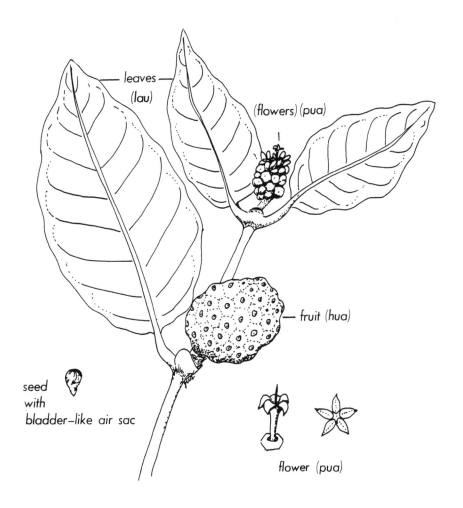

leaves
(lau)

(flowers) (pua)

fruit (hua)

seed
with
bladder–like air sac

flower (pua)

yellow fruit. The ripe fruit measures several inches in diameter. The outside of the fruit is marked by a pattern of shapes. Each tiny shape may have five sides (pentagon), or it may have six sides (hexagon).

The flesh of the fruit is white-yellow. It has an unpleasant taste, and it may smell bad as well.

The seeds (kernels) are oblong, triangular, and red-brown. Each seed has an air sac attached to it. This **bladder** of air on the seed allows it to float on breezes very easily. Because of this **flotation**, the *noni* is a widely **distributed** plant.

POEM:

NONI's leaves are big and shiny,
    With a waxy look,
When pounded with the bark of stems,
    Made tonic people took.

The inner bark of roots can make
    A pretty yellow dye,
Add coral lime and it turns red,
    Something you can try.

Julie Williams

USES:

Only during **famine** did the ancient Hawaiians eat the *noni* fruit. They noticed that cooked *noni* fruit did not have such a disagreeable taste, but they also ate *noni* raw.

The Hawaiians found that the *noni* could act as a poultice to bring boils to a head. The leaves and stem bark of the *noni* were boiled and used as a tonic. If a Hawaiian had lice on his scalp, he would first apply the juice from the *noni* plant to kill them and then wash his head with a coconut shampoo.

The root of the *noni* also provided the Hawaiians with dyes. If they boiled the root with lime made from coral, the Hawaiians could get a red dye. A yellow dye could also be extracted from the root of the *noni*.

LEGEND:

Several Polynesian stories tell of heroes an heroines who were driven to live on the *noni* in days of famine. When Kamapua'a, the pig god who loved Pele, was taunting her, he chanted:

"I have seen the woman gathering *noni*,
Scratching *noni*
Pounding *noni*."

In some way the words conveyed the meaning that Pele, the volcano goddess, had red eyes. This so angered her that she plunged into battle with him.

COMMON NAME:	**True Kou**
HAWAIIAN NAME:	**KOU**

HABITAT:

Kou prefers the warm, sunny areas on the leeward lowlands. It grows **readily** from seeds.

DESCRIPTION:

Kou is a member of the Heliotrope family. It is an evergreen tree which grows about thirty feet tall. The straight trunk of *kou* gives the tree an erect look. This trunk is pale gray with a **grooved** and flaky bark. Over this straight trunk rises a **dense** crown of leaves. Because this crown has a wide spread, the *kou* provides much shade.

From the trunk comes a soft wood that is also **durable.** The wood has beautiful markings and color, such as wavy dark and light lines and bands of yellow.

The leaves of *kou* are smooth. They can have a wavy edge, a rounded base, and a short-pointed tip. Leaves will grow from one-half to three inches long.

Kou bears orange flowers in clusters. *Kou* flowers will be one to two inches in diameter and have five to seven lobes. These flowers have no scent at all.

Kou also bears dry, hard fruit about one inch long.

50

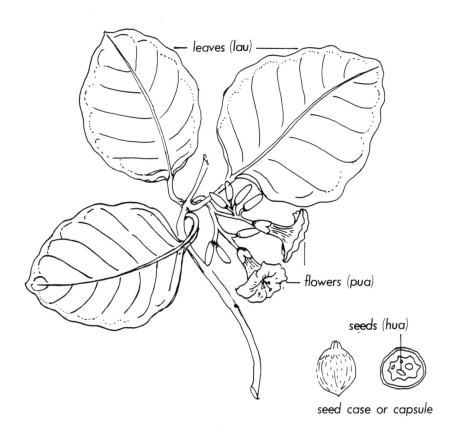

leaves (lau)

flowers (pua)

seeds (hua)

seed case or capsule

The mature fruit is green or yellow and contains a "stone" with one to four seeds. Leaves shaped like a cup enclose the fruit.

POEM:

Prized for their wood
   Were the lovely KOU trees,
Great beauty of grain,
   Cut and carved with such ease.

Calabashes, platters, and dishes for meat,
   Images of gods made skillfully neat.
In the shade of KOU sat women each day,
   Beating their kapa or stringing a lei.

Julie Williams

USES:

Hawaiian women liked to sit in the shade of the *kou* tree when they prepared *kapa*. There they found coolness for their work.

In the Hawaiian household, the *kou* had many uses. The Hawaiians carved the beautiful wood of the *kou*. They found the wood easy to carve. The grain of the *kou* made beautiful calabashes, platters, and bowls. There was no unpleasant sap in the *kou* wood to flavor the food. Fishhook containers and images of the gods were also carved from *kou* wood.

The leaves of the *kou* gave the Hawaiians a red-brown dye. This dye was used for the designs on the *kapa*.

The flowers of *kou* were suitable for leis. Though they have no scent, the small orange flowers looked nice in the Hawaiians' leis.

LEGEND:

In Hawai'i, at 'Ewa, O'ahu, a recorded legend tells of a chiefess who saw an old woman stringing a lei of *kou* blossoms. In a teasing mood the girl said, "Let me have the lei."

The old woman answered angrily, "Youth is asking the old lady for the lei. Go and get flowers and make yourself a lei."

The chiefess bathed and returned and asked again for the lei. She received an angrier reply. She bathed again and sat on the beach, letting her beautiful hair, which was black, hang into the water, and asked yet another time for the lei.

Now, the old woman was a *kahuna*, and she caused sharks to materialize. The sharks called out, "Her hair hangs into the water! What shall we do?"

"Whatever you wish," replied the old woman.

The sharks ate the girl and scattered her blood over the bank, where to this day the soil is red. And to this day no one wears *kou* flowers in that section of 'Ewa.

COMMON NAME:	# Milo
HAWAIIAN NAME:	# MILO

HABITAT:

Milo grew around Hawaiians' houses, never in the forests.

DESCRIPTION:

Milo is a member of the Hibiscus family. This tree grows forty feet tall with a trunk about two feet in diameter. The bark is thick and **corrugated.** The branches of *milo* are widely spread, usually in a **horizontal** direction from the trunk.

Milo has leaves shaped like hearts. The glossy leaves grow from three to five inches across.

Flowers bloom on *milo* during most of the year. These flowers **resemble** small bells, two to three inches in diameter. They have yellow petals and a purple center. During the day, the flowers **wither** and turn purplish-pink.

The fruit of the *milo* bears woody seed cases of five cells. The seed cases are only one inch in diameter and are covered with down (fine, short hair). Only the fruit of trees planted in dry areas will ripen.

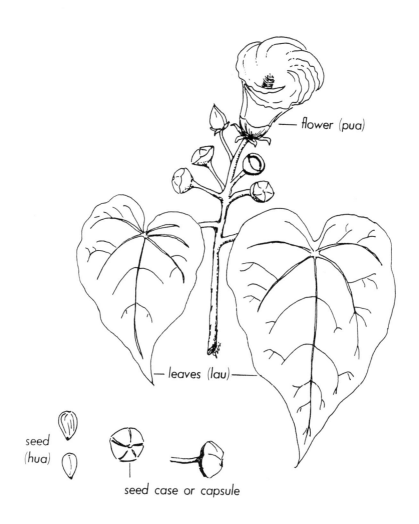

flower (pua)

leaves (lau)

seed
(hua)

seed case or capsule

POEM:

> Lining the path to Waimea's door,
>> Are MILO trees along the shore;
> In forests MILO's never found,
>> Buoyant seeds float to seaside ground.
>
> Beautifully grained, its rich brown wood
>> For food bowls, just like KOU, is good;
> No funny tasting sap to fear,
>> Bright yellow flow'rs most of the year.

Julie Williams

Milo MILO   55

USES:

Milo is popular because it gives shade. Its wood gives no unpleasant taste to food, so the Hawaiians also made calabashes and plates from *milo*. These plants showed the beauty of the *milo* wood grain.

Parts of *milo* gave dye, medicine, oil, and gum to the Hawaiians. The inner bark of the tree gave them fiber and cordage.

The ancient Hawaiians found the young leaves of *milo* to be **edible.**

| COMMON NAME: | # Mountain Apple |
| HAWAIIAN NAME: | # `OHI`A-`AI |

POEM:

> Mountain apple: `ŌHI`A `AI,
>> A forest tree quite tall,
> Tufted flowers of magenta-pink,
>> A carpet when they fall.

> Crisp, pure white pulp, a large round seed,
>> Fruit's thin skin red or white;
> For houseposts and for rafters, too,
>> `Ōhi`a's wood is right.

Julie Williams

HABITAT:

Mountain Apple *('Ohi'a-'ai)* grows in shady valleys up to an altitude of 1800 feet.

DESCRIPTION:

Mountain Apple *('Ohi'a-'ai)* belongs to the Myrtle family. Groves of mountain apple may grow to a height of fifty feet. These trees are very attractive. When *'ohi'a-'ai* grows alone, however, it may be as small as a shrub.

The trunk of *'ohi'a-'ai* is covered with a smooth, spotted gray bark. *'Ohi'a-'ai* has oval leaves. They are shiny and dark green.

From short stems on the trunk and on the heavy branches of *'ohi'a-'ai* grow bright red-purple flowers. These flowers have many **tufts.**

Fruit begins to grow from *'ohi'a-'ai* when the tree is seven or eight years old. The skin of the fruit is very thin. It has a deep crimson color. The inside of *'ohi'a-'ai* fruit is crisp and white. This pulp tastes refreshing and sweet. The skin and the pulp surround a large, round seed.

USES:

The Hawaiians of old ate small amounts of the raw *'ohi'a-'ai* fruit. They preferred to dry it to eat later.

With the wood of the mountain apple *('ohi'a-'ai)*, the Hawaiians built beams for their houses *(hale)*. From the bark they made medicine.

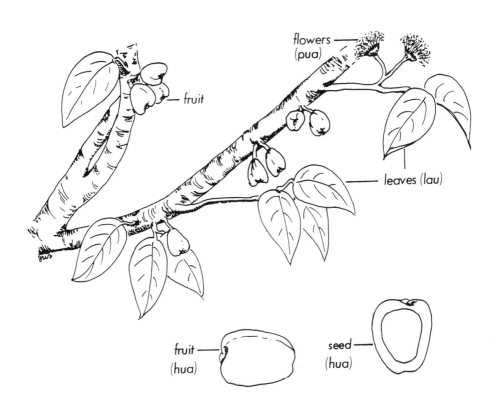

flowers
(pua)

fruit

leaves (lau)

fruit
(hua)

seed
(hua)

Mountain Apple
'OHI'A-'AI

COMMON NAME:	# Paper Mulberry
HAWAIIAN NAME:	# WAUKE

HABITAT:

We find *Wauke* growing in woods or hollows. It grows in moist lands such as along streams, in wet lands, and in dry taro patches. *Wauke* needs protection from the wind.

DESCRIPTION:

Paper Mulberry *(wauke)* is a member of the Fig family. It is a small tree or shrub, but in some regions it grows as tall as fifty feet.

Wauke has leaves shaped like hearts. The upper surface of the leaves is rough, but the lower surface feels wooly. The edges of the leaves are finely **serrated.** A leaf may measure four to six inches long and three to five inches wide.

The flowers of *wauke* have round heads about one inch in diameter. They are fuzzy with long **stigmas** and hairy **bracts.**

Wauke produces round orange fruit, about an inch in diameter.

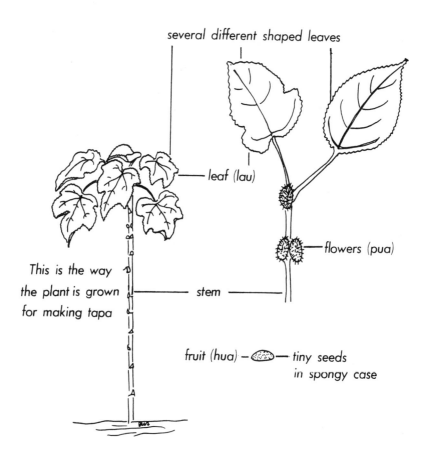

several different shaped leaves

leaf (lau)

flowers (pua)

This is the way
the plant is grown
for making tapa

stem

fruit (hua) — tiny seeds
in spongy case

POEM:

The inner bark of WAUKE
Is used for kapa cloth,
The softest and most durable,
Safe from any moth.

Julie Williams

USES:

The ancient Hawaiians made the finest *kapa* from the **bast** fiber of *wauke*. Do you know what the word *kapa* means? *Ka* means "the." *Pa* means "beaten." Let's find out why this was a good name for the cloth that Hawaiians used for their clothing.

When the *wauke* had grown to the right size, it was cut down. The roots and the top were cut off. The best strips of *wauke* were about three to four feet long and as thick as a man's finger. The bark of these rods was then slit from the top to the bottom. The bark was peeled away from the rods and was carried to some running water. Heavy stones were placed on top of each strip. Do you know why?

When the *wauke* was thoroughly soaked, the women would use a shell and scrape away all the outer green bark. Between much scrapping and dipping the *wauke* in water over and over, nothing remained but the fine fibers of the inner bark. It was a difficult job done only by the women. But this was just the first step in preparing the *wauke*.

These strips were then spread into two or three layers. The women were very careful to make all the cloth into the same thickness. If any part of a piece of bark had been scraped too thin, another thin piece was laid over it. This helped to make the whole piece of *kapa* of the same thickness. This was left until a large proportion of the water had drained off or had evaporated. The fibers began to stick together, so that *kapa* could be lifted from the ground without dropping into pieces.

Can you believe that a piece of cloth could be eleven or twelve feet long, but not more than one foot wide?

Now the *wauke* was ready for "beating." The women would lay it on a long piece of wood *(kau kuku)*. One side of this wood was even and flat. On this side the women placed the *wauke* cloth. The women then began to beat this with a *kapa* beater. There were different types of *tapa* beaters and each was used for a special job. They continued this beating, keeping time with their strokes. The cloth would begin to expand under these strokes. They would double the piece several times, and beat it out again. The *kapa* was then put out into the sun to dry. The sun and the air made the *kapa* very white in a short time.

Both men and women wore clothing made from *wauke kapa*. Their bed sheets as well were made from this *kapa*. The Hawaiians also used *kapa* from *wauke* for certain ceremonies.

The Hawaiians could twist the raw bark of *wauke* to fom a cord. With this cord they made fishnets and carrying nets *(koko)*. Cord from *wauke* helped the Hawaiians to hang or transport calabashes, gourds, and wood. The cord made strong slings or handles for these objects.

The Hawaiians also made a medicine from *wauke*. The slimy sap of *wauke* became a mild **laxative**. To treat thrush *('ea)*, a disease of the mouth, the Hawaiians used the ash from burned *kapa* made from *wauke*.

LEGEND:

Remember that legend tells how a god or goddess who has lived on earth takes at death the form of some plant.

"Of Maikohā, banished son of Konikonia, the myth says that he wandered away and died at Kaupō on Maui and out of his body grew a *wauke* plant of the hairy kind and useful for beating out bark cloth."*

---

*Martha Beckwith, *Hawaiian Mythology* (Honolulu, Hawaii: University of Hawaii Press, 1940), page 99.

Sugar Cane

KŌ

HABITAT:

Sugar cane *(kō)* will grow in the lowlands or at higher elevations. *Kō* planted in the lowlands will **mature** in twelve to fifteen months. Those crops of sugar cane *(kō)* planted at higher elevations will take eighteen to twenty-four months to mature.

DESCRIPTION:

Sugar cane *(kō)* belongs to the Grass family. It grows six to fifteen feet tall on straight stalks. The diameter of the stalk is only one to two inches. The *kō* stalk has clearly marked **internodes** and very hard, thick skin. Inside the stem we find **fibrous** material. The **interior** of the mature *kō* stem is full of sugar juice.

In a field of sugar cane *(kō)*, we see very tall stalks leaning to one side. In high winds the stalks may lean almost to the ground.

Sugar cane *(kō)* bears green leaves. Each leaf has a **midrib**. These leaves may cluster at the top of the stalk. Leaves at the lower part of the stalk die, become dry, and hang down.

In November or December we will see *kō* bloom. It forms a tassel which resembles a feather. The one-to-

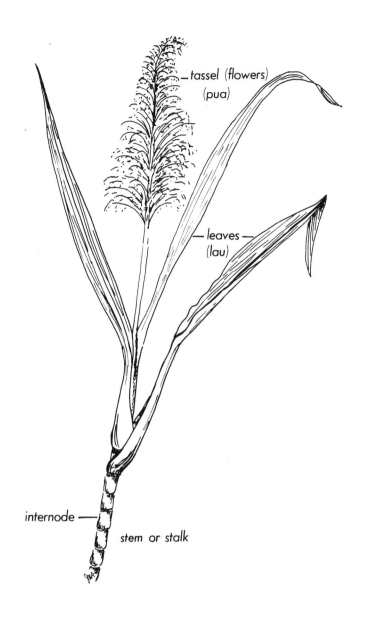

tassel (flowers)
(pua)

leaves
(lau)

internode

stem or stalk

two foot long tassel is sometimes called the "Hawaiian Christmas tree."

Sugar plantations would like to keep the *kō* from blossoming because there is more sugar in a stalk with no tassel. The plantations have been experimenting to find a way to stop the blossoming.

Sugar cane *(kō)* is a **carbohydrate,** a sugar.

POEM:

Sweetest of all Hawaiian foods
Is KŌ, our sugar cane,
It sweetens haupia and kūlolo
And medicines for pain.

Julie Williams

USES:

The Hawaiians used *kō* as a food. On long journeys they carried a stalk of *kō* to relieve **gnawings** of hunger. Children chewed the stalk between meals. The *kō's* sweet pleased the Hawaiians, and the chewing made their teeth strong, they believed.

From the stalk, the Hawaiians extracted juice. They roasted the juice over an open fire. Then they fed it to nursing babies, or they sweetened desserts with it. The sweetness of *kō* also helped cover up the bitter taste of medicines made from herbs.

Lightweight game darts were made from sugar cane tassels *(pua)* cut into two-foot lengths and the flowerets removed. These stalks were straightened by winding the base with a cord to form a clay coating. This game was called *ke'a pua*. It was played during the *Makahiki* season as the sugar cane blooms at this time. This meant that there was much material available to make the darts.

RIDDLES:

"The sugar cane is growing white," is a tactful way of saying that one is growing old.

"The sugar cane *(kō)* flowers." Time for the squid to appear. *(pua ke kō - ku mai ka he'e)*

"When the sugar cane tassels, gather at the sledding course," refers to the grassy hillsides that were used in this sport.

COMMON NAME:	# Sweet Potato
HAWAIIAN NAME:	# 'UALA

HABITAT:

The sweet potato *('uala)* grows in dry areas not good for taro *(kalo)*. We can find *'uala* in low areas and in higher areas up to 5,000 feet of elevation.

DESCRIPTION:

Sweet potato *('uala)* is a member of the Morning Glory family. Most *'uala* are vines growing close to the ground.

The leaf shape of *'uala* varies. Some leaves are heart shaped, but some have five deep **lobes.** *'Uala* will produce pink-lavender flowers. The petals of this flower will form a tube at their base. At the top of the flower, the petals will spread widely apart.

We **cultivate** the sweet potato plant *('uala)* for food. The roots of *'uala* form large **tubers.** These tubers are the sweet potatoes which we like to eat. With each plant, the color of the flesh and skin of the tubers will vary. The sweet potato tuber is a **carbohydrate.**

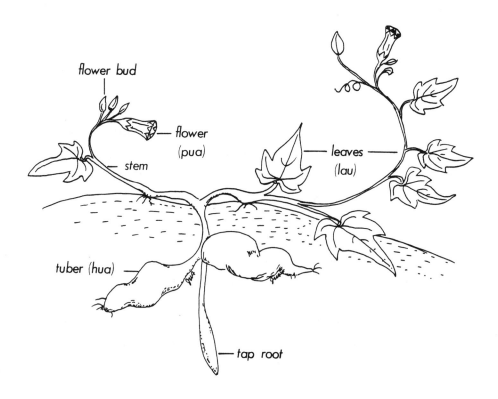

flower bud

flower (pua)

stem

leaves (lau)

tuber (hua)

tap root

POEM:

In Hawai`i sweet potato
      Has the name `UALA,
For its god, whom we all know,
      It has Kamapua`a.

So many, many varieties,
      Two hundred some I'm told,
Tubers and leaves the imu cooked,
      Eaten hot or cold.

Old vines and leaves for soft, soft padding
      Underneath the mat,
Tubers cooked and vines quite fresh
      For pigs so they'd get fat.

Julie Williams

USES:

The ancient Hawaiians also grew the sweet potato *('uala)* for food. Sometimes they ate the tubers raw; sometimes they baked them in an *imu. 'Uala* often served as the starch of the Hawaiians' meal. It could also be mixed with water to make sweet potato poi. The young leaves near the tip of the *'uala* vine could be cooked. The Hawaiians ate these as a green vegetable with their meals. For the hogs, too, the vines and leaves of the sweet potato became a food.

'Uala also served the Hawaiians as a medicine. Sometimes a Hawaiian needed to get rid of something bad he had eaten; then he ate a certain part of the *'uala* to make him vomit.

The sweet potato *('uala)* could also cure **asthma,** serve as a **laxative,** or become a gargle for a sore throat. One type of tuber *(pu)* became bait for fishing.

LEGENDS:

The god of the sweet potato *('uala)* was Kamapua'a. "Kama" is a person or man, "pua'a" is a pig. This god had a snoutlike nose which made it possible for him to dig up sweet potato tubers.

Hina-i-ka-malama found a sweet potato *('uala)* from the moon. This kind was called *hua-lani* (fruit of heaven). Legend says, therefore, that she was "nourished on the moon" *('ai-ka-mālama)*.

When she escaped to the moon, her husband cut off her foot to use as a planting. He wanted to keep this precious new food. She became a goddess and her spirit took the form of the sweet potato *('uala)*.

COMMON NAME:	**Taro**
HAWAIIAN NAME:	**KALO**

POEM:

> Three hundred kinds of KALO,
>   Grown by na mahi`ai,
> In uplands or in flooded ponds,
>   Where flows the fresh, cold wai.
>
> The starchy tubers first are steamed,
>   Then pounded into poi,
> The cooked leaves eaten as lū`au,
>   Good for each girl and boy.

Julie Williams

HABITAT:

Wet taro needs a marshy place to grow; dry taro grows in moist uplands.

DESCRIPTION:

Taro *(kalo)* is a member of the Arum family. It grows a foot or more tall. Its leaves grow in an upright cluster. These leaves are shaped somewhat like arrowheads.

Taro *(kalo)* bears a short underground stem called a corm. Here the plant stores starch produced by the leaves. The corm swells as it stores more and more starch. It can grow to a great size; in the eight to sixteen months of its development, the corm can grow as large as six inches in diameter. People raise taro *(kalo)* to obtain this valuable starchy root.

When the plant reaches **maturity,** it will produce a flower stalk. This flower stalk is not as tall as the leaf stalks. Near the **apex** of the flower stalk stalk appears the **spathe.** The **spathe,** or modified leaf, covers and protects the flower cluster within. Inside we will find an erect stem, the **spadix.** The **spadix** bears two kinds of flowers: the "male" and the "female" flowers. The male flowers lie forward toward the upper part of the **spadix,** and the female flowers lie toward the lower part.

Chewing the raw taro *(kalo)* plant will be very painful to the mouth. The lining of the mouth is **irritated** by needle-shaped crystals of calcium oxalate which fill the cells of *kalo.* When we bite the raw plant cells or wet them with our saliva, they release the crystals of calcium oxalate. To test how painful these crystals are, touch the tongue very gently to the cut end of the stem. Fortunately, cooking will dissolve these **minute** crystals. Therefore, we can eat the cooked *kalo* without feeling any pain.

It is said that insects and **herbivorous** animals will stay

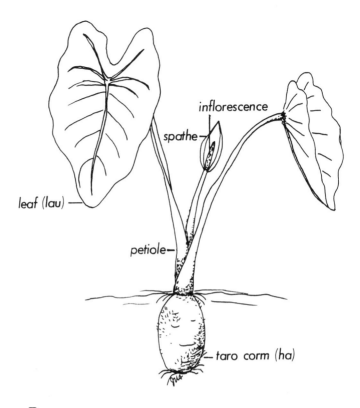

inflorescence

spathe

leaf (lau)

petiole

taro corm (ha)

Taro

KALO

away from taro *(kalo)*. Therefore, farmers do not have to worry about injury to their plants from insects or animals. Do you think that they avoid taro because of the crystals of calcium oxalate?

Taro *(kalo)* is considered the staple of the Hawaiians. It was one of the most important foods grown by the Hawaiians. Even today people consider taro *(kalo)* a very healthful food. Many babies who are allergic to milk grow strong and healthy when they are given poi made from taro. Taro is a **carbohydrate**, a starch.

There are over 275 different types of taro *(kalo)* that have evolved from the first taro that the Polynesians brought to Hawai'i. The Hawaiians grew taro in two ways:

1. Wet land taro was grown in a *lo'i*, an **artificial** paddy or marsh called a taro *(kalo)* patch.
2. Dry land taro was planted in soil not flooded, usually in forested areas. There was a high rainfall here, so the taro *(kalo)* did not need irrigation.

USES:

The Hawaiians relied upon taro *(kalo)* for food. From the corm the Hawaiians pounded poi, the Hawaiian "staff of life" or staple. They had many other special recipes for this tuber. For example, the Hawaiians cooked unpounded taro to make *kalo pa'a*, and they steamed or baked grated taro with coconut cream to make *kūlolo*, a pudding.

The Hawaiians cooked the **immature** leaves of the plant in water or steamed them. The leaves served as the greens for their meals. Sometimes the Hawaiians cooked the *kalo* leaves with coconut milk *(wai'a ka niu)* in a leaf packet *(laulau)*. They also boiled the cut stems for a vegetable. Some of the Hawaiians preferred to peel the stems first.

As a medicine, the taro *(kalo)* served the Hawaiians well. They rubbed raw corm on their wounds to stop the bleeding. Their rubbing the raw stem leaf **(petiole)** on insect bites prevented swelling and pain. The raw juice of taro *(kalo)* could be mixed with other juices to reduce fever. Also as a cure for thrush *('ea)*, the Hawaiians grated the corm and mixed it with the ash of burnt coconut *(niu)* meat. The Hawaiians used hard poi from *kalo* as a **poultice** on infected sores.

NAMES OF VARIETIES:

Here are some of the names the Hawaiians gave to taro varieties.

A. They named these for their shapes:
1. *'api'i* - ruffled leaf
2. *'apuwai* - cup-shaped leaf
3. *lau-loa* - long leaf said to be the original type brought to Hawaii

B. They named these for their colors:
1. *'ele'ele* - blackish color
2. *haokea* - white
3. *poni* - purplish color

C. The ancient Hawaiians named some varieties of taro after fish:
1. *he'e* - a squid
2. *kūmū* - taro *(kalo)* with a bright red stalk that reminded them of the *kūmū.*
3. *humuhumu* - colors and markings of this plant reminded them of the *humuhumu.*
4. *kala* - the *kala* fish
5. *manini* - taro plants with stripes like the *manini.*

D. These names were chosen because the plants reminded the Hawaiians of gods, kings, flowers and birds:
1. *'elepaio* - leaves of this taro have splotches like the markings of the *'elepaio* bird.
2. *hekili* - favorite of Kahekili, king of Maui.
3. *lehua* - had a red corm and *piko* like the *lehua* blossom
4. *pueo ha-lena-lena* - reminded the Hawaiians of an owl
5. *uahi-a-pele* - smoke of Pele

LEGENDS:

The ancient Hawaiians have a legend that explains one reason some of the plants and animals have the same name:

The demigod Kamapua'a was running away from Pele. Pele and Kamapua'a were always fighting, and this time he wanted to trick her so she couldn't follow him.

First he hid in the sea, but to make it hard for Pele to find him, he turned himself into a *he'e*, then a *manini*, next a *pueo*, and lastly, a *kala*. But Pele went into the sea after him and was catching up.

So Kamapua'a ran to a *Lo'i*. Here he went through the same changes, but this time he had the form of *kalo*. Pele could not follow because her eyes were bleary with salt water.

But to make sure he had really lost her, Kamapua'a ran into the forest. Once more he changed, this time into forest trees called *he'e, manini, pueo* and *kala*.

And this is why there are fish, taro plants and forest trees with the same names.

Hawaiians say *kalo* was brought by Wākea, "Father Heaven" and ancestor of all their chiefs.

A legendary heroine, Hoamakeike, was said to have been born in the form of a taro bulb and thrown into a trash pile. In a vision, her grandmother saw the spirit of the child and she rescued the rainbow-arched bulb, which in two days became a girl child without blemish.

Two beautiful taros *(kalo)* loved each other very much. When a chief pointed them out as food for a feast, they moved to another part of the patch. This happened again and again until in desperation they took wing and flew from taro patch to taro patch; but they were already discovered by the angry chief. Finally, a kindly Hawaiian took pity on them, and in his taro patch they lived to a happy old age.

Much of the taro *(kalo)* of old Hawai'i was said to have been planted by the *menehunes,* the little people who worked only at night.

PROVERBS:

"This one will not be taken by an old taro leaf, but only by the tender bud of the plant." Used in disdain of an older suitor.

"A single roll of cooked taro leaf is delicious if seasoned with affection."

RIDDLES:

Who is the little man with swaying chin, swaying?   —the taro leaf.

My little fish;	He nane
Cut off its head.	Ku'u wahi i'a:
Cut off its tail.	Moku ke Po'o.
Return to the water.	Moku ka Hi'u.
It lives again.	Ho'iho 'I I ka Wai.
What am I?	A Ola hou.

COMMON NAME:	Tī
HAWAIIAN NAME:	KĪ or LĀʻĪ

HABITAT:

Tī (kī) grows on the edges of woods and in wet, open forests at lower elevations. People also plant it around their houses to keep evil spirits away.

DESCRIPTION:

Tī (kī) is a member of the Lily family. Tī is a simple plant with very few branches. It grows three to ten feet high. Its broad, smooth leaves overlap each other at the base. The lower leaves turn yellow and drop from the plant.

From the center of the leaves rises a tall stem. This stem will bear many small branches full of small pink flowers. On some varities of tī (kī), small red or yellow berries will develop from the flowers.

POEM:

So many uses can be made
       Of shiny green-leaved KĪ,
For wrapping laulau, fish, and poi,
       And making lei lāʻi.

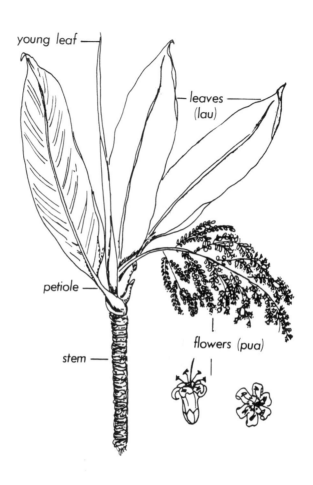

young leaf

leaves
(lau)

petiole

flowers (pua)

stem

For hiding sharp bone hooks
    Upon the cowry octopus lure,
For sandals, rain capes, bandages,
    For headaches it's a cure.

Sacred to god, Lono,
    Offerings made to him,
Grown around the hale,
    Away with spirits grim!

Julie Williams

USES:

The Hawaiians put the tī leaves to great use as wrappers. Before cooking food, the Hawaiians wrapped it in tī *(kī)* leaves. Individual servings of pork or beef and fish, for example, were mixed with taro tops and wrapped in tī leaves for the *imu*. This food is called *laulau*. Fish wrapped in tī *(kī)* leaves and broiled on coals is called *lawalu*. The Hawaiians also wrapped pudding in tī leaves before cooking it.

Wrappers for carrying and storing bundles the Hawaiians called *pu'olo*. A lei could be wrapped and carried in *pu'olo* to keep the flowers fresh.

Tī *(kī)* roots themselves became food for the ancient Hawaiians. With the baked root of tī *(kī)*, the Hawaiians made a sweet candy. They baked the candy in an oven *(kaimuki)*. *Kaimuki* means oven for the tī *(kī)* roots.

Clothing, too, was made from tī *(kī)* leaves. The Hawaiians made sandals, raincoats, and hula skirts from the leaves of *kī*. The tough fibers of the leaves made a sturdy and waterproof protection.

Tī *(kī)* leaves became thatch for the Hawaiians' roofs. The leaves provided shelter for the people inside the *hale*. The Hawaiians planted Tī outside their houses *(hale)* and the *heiau* as well to purify them.

The Hawaiians tied tī *(kī)* leaves along a long rope to make a *hukilau*. With the *hukilau* the Hawaiians herded fish into a circle where they caught the fish.

As a medicine, the tī *(kī)* was also useful. The leaves helped cool the brows of Hawaiians who had a fever; the Hawaiians believe too that the tī *(kī)* would cure a headache. With a young tī *(kī)* leaf, one not yet unfolded, the Hawaiians would bandage a wound. Also, a Hawaiian with a backache would use tī *(kī)* leaves to feel better; he would wrap a warm stone against the sore part of his back with several tī leaves.

LEGENDS:

A king of Kaua'i used a toy canoe made from a tī *(kī)* leaf to make a decision. The floating leaf would show him which of his sons to send on a search for their eldest brother.

Legends also say that once a shark lived in Waipi'o stream. Before a man would dare to swim across the stream, he would throw in a tī *(kī)* stalk. If the stalk disappeared, the shark must be there, he thought. But if the stalk floated downstream, the man would dare to plunge in and swim across.

COMMON NAME:	# Turmeric
HAWAIIAN NAME:	# ʻŌLENA

HABITAT:

Turmeric *(ʻōlena)* grows in damp valleys with a forest.

DESCRIPTION:

Turmeric *(ʻōlena)* belongs to the Ginger family. Like the banana plant, *ʻōlena* has no stem above ground. It does, however, have thick underground stems. The underground stems are orange or yellow on the inside. Bright yellow is the characteristic color of the spice turmeric which we use in our cooking.

In the early months of spring, leaves appear on the turmeric plant; in the fall, the leaves will die. Several leaves grow in a cluster from the underground stem, rising twenty inches or higher from the ground. The **petioles** (leaf stalks) overlap. Because they overlap, *ʻōlena* appears to have a stem. But this is a false stem. The **petioles** each bear a light green blade which measures eight by three inches or larger.

Flowers shaped like a five-inch cylinder come out

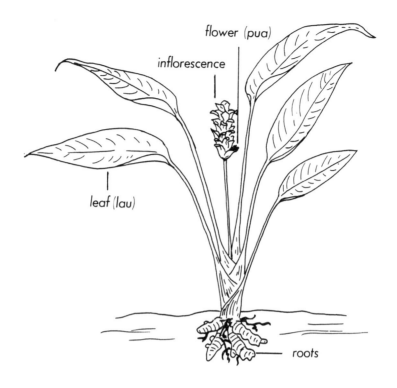

flower (pua)

inflorescence

leaf (lau)

roots

with the leaves. The flower grows on a long stem in the center of the leaf stalks. It is made up of curved **bracts.** From each lower, pale green **bract** grow two or more pale yellow flowers. From the upper **bracts,** which are pink, no flowers grow.

This plant rarely has seeds. A new plant will grow from the sprouting root rather than from seeds. Turmeric (*'ōlena*) is very rare now. In the wild we cannot find these plants easily, but some people cultivate them in their gardens.

POEM:

From yellow bright to orange,
　　`ŌLENA does provide,
By pressing all the juice there is,
　　From the roots inside.

Relieving sinuses and aches
　　That hurt within our ears,
In rituals to purify,
　　To take away all fears.

Julie Williams

USES:

With turmeric *('ōlena)* the Hawaiians made dyes for their tapa *(kapa)*. Different parts of the plant gave them different colors. From the young underground stems, they made a bright yellow dye. By steaming these young stems, they obtained an orange dye. Orange or gold dye came from the **mature** underground stems.

Turmeric *('ōlena)* also served the Hawaiians as a medicine. A lung disease called consumption (tuberculosis) was treated with turmeric. The Hawaiians believed that turmeric *('ōlena)* helped them when they had an earache. They also used turmeric to clear the sinus and to treat a growth in the nose.

COMMON NAME:	**YAM**
HAWAIIAN NAME:	**UHI**

POEM:

UHI's stems are winged and square,
    A vine with tubers big,
Cooked in the imu, eaten hot,
    When cold, fed to a pig.

UHI isn't sweet potato,
    "Yam" is its common name,
Its vine must have support from trees,
    'Uala's not the same.

Julie Williams

HABITAT:

Yam *(uhi)* grows in wet gulches and forests. It climbs on trunks and branches of trees for support.

DESCRIPTION:

Yam *(uhi)* is a member of the Yam family. This plant is a vine; it must have some support to climb.

The stem of the yam is square; it has four flat sides. On opposite sides of the stem grow light green leaves. These leaves are sometimes oval and sometimes heart shaped. They grow three to six inches long. The veins of the leaves all begin in one spot at the base of the leaves.

The flowers of the yam *(uhi)* are small. They have no petals, and they have a green-yellow or yellow **calyx.**

The fruit of the yam *(uhi)* form from the **fertilized** female flower. The underground stem forms a thick tuber. The **tubers** of yam are harvested and eaten. Yam *(uhi)* is a **carboyhydrate,** a starch.

IMPORTANT INFORMATION:

There is one yam *(uhi)* that is poisonous. We can recognize it easily; it has a round stem and its tuber grows above ground.

USES:

The Hawaiians like to cook the yam *(uhi)* in the *imu* and eat it hot. It does not make good poi, for it is too mealy.

The Hawaiians used the yam *(uhi)* as a medicine for a cough.

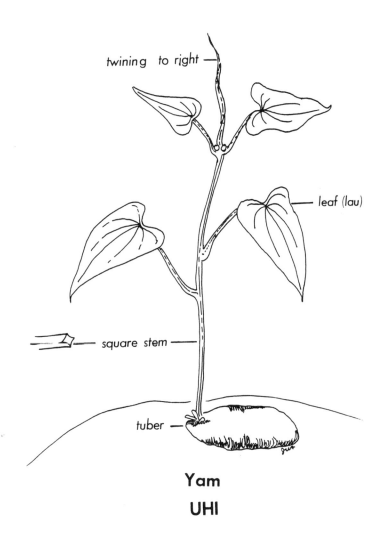

twining to right

leaf (lau)

square stem

tuber

Yam

UHI

Resources For Teachers

Beckwith, Martha. *Hawaiian Mythology*. New Haven: Yale University Press, for Folklore Foundation of Vassar College, 1940. Reprinted by University of Hawaii Press, 1970.

Bryan, Edwin H., Jr. *Ancient Hawaiian Life*. Honolulu, Hawaii: Advertiser Publishing Co., 1938.

Buck, Peter H. (Te Rangi Hiroa) *Arts and Crafts of Hawaii*. Bernice P. Bishop Museum Spec. Pub. No. 45. Honolulu, Hawaii: Bishop Museum Press, 1957. Reprinted in separate sections, 1964.

Degener, Otto. *Ferns and Flowering Plants of Hawaii National Park*. Honolulu, Hawaii: Honolulu Star Bulletin, 1930. Several reprints, latest 1974.

_____. *Plants of Hawaii National Park Illustrative of Plants and Customs of the South Seas*. Ann Arbor, Michigan: Edward Brothers, Inc., 1945.

Feher, Joseph. *Hawaii: A Pictorial History*. Honolulu, Hawaii: Bishop Museum Press, 1969.

Geary, Ida. *Plant Prints & Collages*. New York City, N.Y.: Viking Press, 1978.

Green and Pukui. *Legends of Kawelo and Other Hawaiian Folktales*. Honolulu, Hawaii: University of Hawaii Press, 1936.

Greenwell, Amy B. H. *Economic Botany*. Taro, Volume 1, Number 1, 1947.

Handy, E.S. Craighill. *The Hawaiian Planter,* Volume 1. Bernice P. Bishop Museum Bulletin 161. Honolulu Hawaii: Bernice P. Bishop Museum, 1940. Reprinted by Kraus Reprint Co., New York, N.Y., 1973 or 1974.

_____ and Elizabeth Green. *Native Planters in Old Hawaii.* Bernice P. Bishop Museum Bulletin 233. Honolulu, Hawaii: Bishop Museum Press, 1972.

_____ and Mary Kawena Pukui. *The Polynesian Family System in Ka'u, Hawaii.* Wellington, New Zealand: Polynesian Society, Inc. 1958. Reprinted by Charles E. Tuttle Co., Rutland, Vermont and Tokyo, 1958.

Judd, Henry P. *Hawaiian Proverbs and Riddles.* Bernice P. Bishop Museum Bulletin 77, 1930. Honolulu, Hawaii: Bernice P. Bishop Museum. Reprinted by Kraus Reprint Co., New York, 1971.

Kaaiakamanu, D.M., and J.K. Akina. *Hawaiian Herbs of Medicinal Value.* Honolulu, Hawaii: Board of Health, Territory of Hawaii, 1922. Reprinted by Pacific Book House, 1968; and Charles E. Tuttle Co., Rutland, Vermont and Tokyo, 1973.

Krauss, Beatrice H. *Ethnobotany of Hawaii.* Honolulu, Hawaii: University of Hawaii Press, 1976.

_____. *Ethnobotony of the Hawaiians.* Honolulu, Hawaii: University of Hawaii, Harold L. Lyons Arboretum, 1975.

Larsen, Nils P. *Medical Arts in Ancient Hawaii.* Honolulu, Hawaii. 53rd Annual Report of the Hawaiian Historical Society, 1944.

MacDonald, Gordon A., and Will Kyselka. *Anatomy of an Island.* Honolulu, Hawaii: Bernice P. Bishop Museum Press, 1967.

McBride, L.R. *The Kahuna.* Hilo, Hawaii: The Petroglyph Press, 1972.

Mitchell, Donald D. *Resource Units in Hawaiian Culture.* Honolulu, Hawaii: Kamehameha Schools, 1969.

Neal, Marie. *In Gardens of Hawaii.* Honolulu, Hawaii: Bernice P. Bishop Museum Press, 1965.

Piianaia, Heulu. *A Guide to Hawaiian Culture Units Offered by Na Pono Hawai'i.* Honolulu, Hawaii: Hawaiian Studies Resource Team, Kamehameha Schools, 1969.

Schattenberg, Myrtle. *Medicinal Plants.* Honolulu, Hawaii: Bishop Museum Docent Report, 1974.

Schattenberg, Patricia. *A Guide to Some Plants in Bishop Museum Courtyard.* Honolulu, Hawaii: Botany 450, 1975.

Wise, John Sr. *M.D.* Honolulu, Hawaii: Honolulu Star Bulletin, 1938.

Resources For Children

Aloha Council, Boy Scouts of America. *Hawaiiana*. Aloha Council, Boy Scouts of America, 1973.

Berkey, Helen. *Hawaiian Tales*. Columbus, Ohio: Charles E. Merrill Publishing Co., 1968.

Dunford, Betty. *The Hawaiians of Old*. Honolulu, Hawaii: The Bess Press, 1980.

Hawaiian Treasures in the Exhibition, "Artificial Curiosities of the 18th Century," Honolulu, Hawaii: Bishop Museum, 1978.

Kalo: Man's Kaikua'ana: Why There Are Different Kinds; Kalo in Hawaiian Life; Names for Kalo. Nanakuli Model School Project, Dept. of Education State TAC-T2-5222B-DOE State Office Liliuokalani - E Himeni Hawai'i Kakou.

Mitchell, Donald. *Hawaiian Games for Today*. Honolulu, Hawaii: The Kamehameha Schools Press, 1975.

Pukui, Mary Kawena and Caroline Curtis. *Pikoi and Other Legends of the Island of Hawaii*. Honolulu, Hawaii: The Kamehameha Schools Press, 1971.

_____. *Tales of the Menehune*. Honolulu, Hawaii: The Kamehameha Schools Press, 1971.

_____. *The Water of Kane*. Honolulu, Hawaii: The Kamehameha Schools Press, 1961.

Pukui, Mary Kawena and Samuel Elbert. *Hawaiian Dictionary*. Honolulu, Hawaii: University of Hawaii Press, 1971.

_____. *Place Names of Hawaii*. Honolulu, Hawaii: University of Hawaii Press, 1966.

Selsam, Millicial. *Birth of an Island*. New York, N.Y.: Scholastic Book Service, 1959.

Titcomb, Margaret. *The Ancient Hawaiians*, "How They Clothed Themselves," "Who Were They?" "How Did They Live?" Honolulu, Hawaii: Hogarth Press: 1974.

Diacritical Markings

As you observe the Hawaiian language, you will see that diacritical marking is used consistently. I believe firmly that in any written work a student does with Hawaiian plants, the teacher will do the child a service to guide him toward accurate pronunciation and written spelling. The absence of the hamza (glottal stop or *'okina*) may completely change the meaning of a word. The hamza (') *(or 'okina)* is also necessary for correct pronunciation. It indicates that at one time a consonant appeared in that place and has since been dropped.

The hyphen (-) indicates divisions between the words which make up a name.

In the Hawaiian language "s" is not used to form the plural of a noun.

CONSONANTS:

p, k	about the same as in English but with less aspiration
h, l, m, n	about the same as in English
w	after i and e usually like v;
	after u and o usually like w;
	initially and after a like v or w.
	The *'okina* (glottal stop) is similar to the sound between the "oh's" in English "oh-oh."

VOWELS:

Vowels marked with macrons (ˉ) *(kahakō)* are somewhat longer than other vowels.

a, ā	like a in far
e	like e in bet
ē	like ay in play
i, ī	like ee in see
o, ō	like o in sole
u, ū	like oo in moon

RISING DIPTHONGS:

ei, eu, oi, ou, ai, ae, ao, au

These are always stressed on the first phoneme, but the two phonemes are not as closely joined as in English.

STRESS OR ACCENT:

On all the vowels with macrons *(kahakō):*

ā, ē, ī, ō, ū.

Glossary

A

abrasive *adj.* causing abrasion; scraping or rubbing. *n.* something that grinds, scrapes or polishes.

aerial *adj.* of or in the air.

allergy *n.* a condition in which one becomes sick by breathing in, touching, eating, etc. some particular substance that is not harmful to most people.

altitude *n.* height; especially the height of a thing above the earth's surface or above sea level.

angular *adj.* having angles or sharp corners.

apex *n.* the highest point of anything.

artificial *adj.* made by man, not by nature; not natural.

asthma *n.* a disease in which there are attacks of wheezing, coughing and hard breathing.

B

bast *n.* a strong fiber gotten from plants and used in making ropes and mats.

bladder *n.* a part like a bag inside the body that collects fluid.

bract *n.* a leaf that grows at the base of a flower or on the flower stem. Bracts usually look like small scales.

C

calyx *n.* the outer ring of leaves, or sepals, growing at the base of a flower. It forms the outer cover of the unopened bud.

carbohydrate *n.* any of a group of substances made up of carbon, hydrogen, and oxygen, including sugars and starches.

cathartic *n.* a strong medicine to make the bowels move, as in castor oil.

catkin *n.* the blossom of certain trees consisting of a cluster of small flowers along a drooping spike.

characteristic *adj.* that helps make up the special character of some person or thing.

collector *n.* a person or thing that collects.

common *adj.* belonging equally to each or all.

composite *adj.* made up of distinct parts; compound; (the head of a *composite* flower, as the aster, is made up of many small flowers).

congest *v.* to make too full; make crowded; (congestion, *n.*).

corm *n.* an underground stem of certain plants that looks like a bulb (the taro grows from a corm).

corrugate *v.* to form ridges and furrows in, so as to give a wavy surface.

crescent *n.* the shape of the moon in its first or last quarter; anything shaped like this:

cultivate *v.* to prepare and use land for growing crops.

D

debris *n.* broken, scattered remains; rubbish.

delicacy *n.* condition of being delicate; fineness in skill or work; fragile beauty, sensitiveness.

dense *adj.* having its parts close together; crowded; thick.

diacritical mark *adj. and n.* a mark added to a letter to show how to pronounce it; example: 'o, ā

diagram *n.* a drawing, plan, or chart that helps explain a thing by showing all its parts.

diameter *n.* a straight line passing through the center of a circle or sphere, as in the distance from one side of a tree trunk to the other.

diarrhea *n.* a condition in which bowel movements come too often and are too loose.

distribute *v.* to give out in shares; deal out.

dress *n.* i.e., dressing, *adj.* to size, as of leather or a surfboard.

droop *v.* to sink, hang or bend down.

drupe *n.* a soft, fleshy fruit enclosing a hard-shelled stone or seed.

dysentery *n.* a disease of the intestines, in which there are loose bowel movements containing blood and mucus.

E

edible *adj.* fit to be eaten.

elliptical *adj.* shaped like an oval.

evolve *v.* to develop by gradual change.

expel *v.* to drive out or throw out with force; eject.

extract *v.* to get by squeezing, pressure, etc.

exude *v.* to come or pass out in drops; ooze.

F

famine *n.* a great lack of food that causes starving throughout a wide region; or starvation.

fertilize *v.* to bring a male germ cell to a female egg cell so as to cause a new animal or plant to develop.

fiber *n.* any of the thin parts like threads that form tissue of a plant.

fibrous *adj.* made up of fibers.

flotage *n.* the act or state of floating.

flotation *n.* see flotage.

friction *n.* rubbing one thing against another.

fringe *n.* a border or an outside edge.

G

glottal stop: a sound produced in the larynx by instantaneous closure of the glottis as at the beginning of a cough, or as in the pronouncing of bottle. English does not have this.

gnaw *v.* to bite or wear bit by bit.

groove *n.* a long and narrow hollow, cut or worn into a surface.

H

habitat *n.* the place where an animal or a plant is normally found.

herbivorous *adj.* that eats mainly grass or other plants.

horizontal *adj.* parallel to the horizon; level, flat.

I

identity *n.* that by which we are known. A being the same or exactly alike.

immature *adj.* not mature, not fully grown.

impenetrable *adj.* that which cannot be passed through.

incline *v.* to lean, slope or slant.

inferior *adj.* not so good as something else.

interior *n.* the inside or inner part.

invert *v.* to turn upside down.

L

laxative *adj.* making the bowels move. —*n.* a medicine that does this.

legend *n.* **1.** a story handed down through the years and connected with some real events, but probably not true in itself. **2.** all such stories as a group. **3.** a title or description or key under a picture, map or chart.

literal *adj.* based on actual words in their usual meaning.

lobe *n.* a rounded part that sticks out.

louse *n.* a small insect pest that lives in hair or on the skin of man and sucks his blood.

lure *v.* to attract or lead by offering something that seems pleasant; entice. —*n.* **1.** anything that lures. **2.** an artificial bait used in fishing.

luxuriant *adj.* growing thick and healthy; lush.

M

macron *n.* the mark -, used over a vowel to show how it is pronounced and in some cases to indicate the plural as well.

margin *n.* a border or edge.

mature *adj.* fully grown or developed.

midrib *n.* the middle vein of a leaf.

minute *adj.* very small, tiny.

model *n.* **1.** a small copy of something. **2.** a small figure made to serve as the plan for the final, larger thing. **3.** a person or thing that ought to be imitated.

mottle *v.* to mark with spots or blotches or different colors.

N

narcotic *n.* a drug that causes deep sleep and lessens pain.

non-, a prefix meaning "not."

nourishment *n.* something that feeds or provides the things needed for life and growth; food.

P

percussion *n.* a hitting of one thing against another.

petiole *n.* the stem by which a leaf is attached to a plant.

plait *n.* a braid; —*v.* to braid something, like hair.

poultice *n.* a soft, wet mixture put on a sore or inflamed part of the body.

R

readily *adv.* to do easily, willingly.

receptacle *n.* anything used to keep something in.

resemble *v.* to be like or look like.

respiratory *adj.* having to do with breathing.

S

scallop *n.* to cut in scallops.

serrate (or **serrated**) *adj.* having notches like teeth of a saw along the edge; as, a serrate leaf.

sleuth *n.* a detective.

spadix *n.* a spike or a head of flowers with a fleshy axis, usually enclosed within a spathe.

sparingly *adv.* of spare, small in amount, meager, scanty.

spathe *n.* a large bract or pair of bracts sheathing a flower cluster.

spiral *adj.* circling around a center in a flat or rising curve that keeps growing larger or smaller.

staple *n.* the main product of a certain place; any article of food that is regularly used and kept in large amounts.

stigma *n.* the upper tip of the pistil of a flower, where pollen settles to make seeds grow.

strand *n.* a shore or a beach.

sucker *n.* a shoot growing from the roots or lower stem of a plant.

T

tan *n.* to preserve.

tendril *n.* a small, curly stem that holds up a climbing plant by coiling around something.

tonic *adj.* giving strength or energy.

tuber *n.* a short, thick part of an underground stem, as a potato.

tuft *n.* a bunch of hairs, feathers, grass, threads, etc. growing or tied closely together.

V

vein *n.* any of the fine lines, or ribs, in a leaf.

W

wither *v.* to dry up; shrivel.